Led Zeppelin

Rock Icons

Publisher's Note: Readers will note that the sharpness of the images in this book varies. This is to be expected of photography from this era and of this nature. Images have been chosen not just for their quality, but also for their atmosphere, intimacy and evocative insight into Led Zeppelin's history.

Publisher and Creative Director: Nick Wells

Commissioning Editor: Polly Prior

Art Director: Mike Spender

Layout Design: Jane Ashley

Digital Design & Production: Chris Herbert

Special thanks to: Anna Groves, Dawn Laker and Catherine Taylor

FLAME TREE PUBLISHING

6 Melbray Mews, Fulham

London SW6 3NS

United Kingdom

www.flametreepublishing.com

www.flametreemusic.com

This edition first published 2019

A CIP record for this book is available from the British Library upon request.

ISBN: 978-1-78755-735-2

Printed in China

Led Zeppelin
Rock Icons

HUGH FIELDER

Foreword by Dave Lewis

FLAME TREE PUBLISHING

Contents

Foreword

Tribute bands treading the boards nightly all over the globe; film producers always on the lookout to use their songs as soundtracks; tattoo artists for ever being requested by fans to etch those four iconic symbols onto willing arms; a catalogue of music constantly played on the radio, downloaded and streamed. For a band that was together a mere 12 years, the fascination for all things Led Zeppelin remains immense.

The chemistry of the four members was, of course, just perfect. Jimmy Page, the relentless riff architect and sonic producer. Robert Plant: silver-throated vocalist with the golden-god, front-man appeal. John Paul Jones: supremely talented bassist and keyboardist – a man for all seasons and all instruments. John Bonham: a thunderous but incisive percussionist who knew exactly when to lay on and off the beat.

Under the maverick management of Peter Grant, they flaunted regular rock business convention in a way that allowed them total artistic freedom. With it came a hedonistic on-the-road lifestyle that remains almost as legendary as the music they created. With their solid rock foundation as a springboard, they interwove blues, folk, funk, jazz, country, jug band and Eastern influences, making every style their own. Live on stage, they constantly slayed audiences with lengthy and compelling performances, while their elaborate album covers added to the whole mystique of the band. Fifty years on from their formation, Led Zeppelin remain very much in the present tense and they continue to cast a giant shadow over the musical landscape. This book unravels the story behind the legend.

Dave Lewis

Editor of the Led Zeppelin magazine and website *Tight But Loose* (www.tightbutloose.co.uk)

The Power and the Glory

No band has exerted power the way Led Zeppelin did. And no band has ever been as powerful as Led Zeppelin.

Power Over the Record Company

They exerted power over their record company. Before Led Zeppelin, record companies could dictate what a band released and when they released it. Even The Beatles and the Rolling Stones had their British albums routinely filleted and reconfigured by their American labels. Tracks were arbitrarily removed and singles and B-sides – which the bands had explicitly refused to put on an album – were inserted. In this way American record companies were able to turn six British albums into nine American albums. And there was nothing the bands could do about it.

Led Zeppelin offered Atlantic Records in New York the opportunity to release their records worldwide. In return they demanded – and got – complete control over their albums, from the musical content to the cover. No band had ever done this before.

Power Over the Promoter

They exerted power over their live performances. Before Led Zeppelin, bands generally received around 50 per cent of the attendance receipts. The rest was split between the promoter, the agent and the venue owner. Once Led Zeppelin were big enough to fill any venue, they demanded

'Led Zeppelin are my favourite rock band. They sound like people who know how to have sex.'

GEORGE MICHAEL

– and got – 90 per cent of the gate receipts, leaving the promoter to make their profit from the remaining 10 per cent. No band had ever done this before. At the height of their power, they were hiring the venue and then hiring the promoter to stage the show.

Musical Power

None of this would have been possible without Led Zeppelin's music, which exerted a power of its own. They took a harder style of blues-rock music that was growing in popularity and doubled down on it. And then they wiped the floor with the opposition. On their first American tour they played anywhere they could for whatever the promoter offered them. By the end of that tour, no headline band wanted to go on after Led Zeppelin. From their second tour onwards they were the headline act.

Power Over Their Rivals

They could do all this because of the power of their music. They sold more albums than any of their rivals. They sold more concert tickets than any of their rivals. In 1973, they

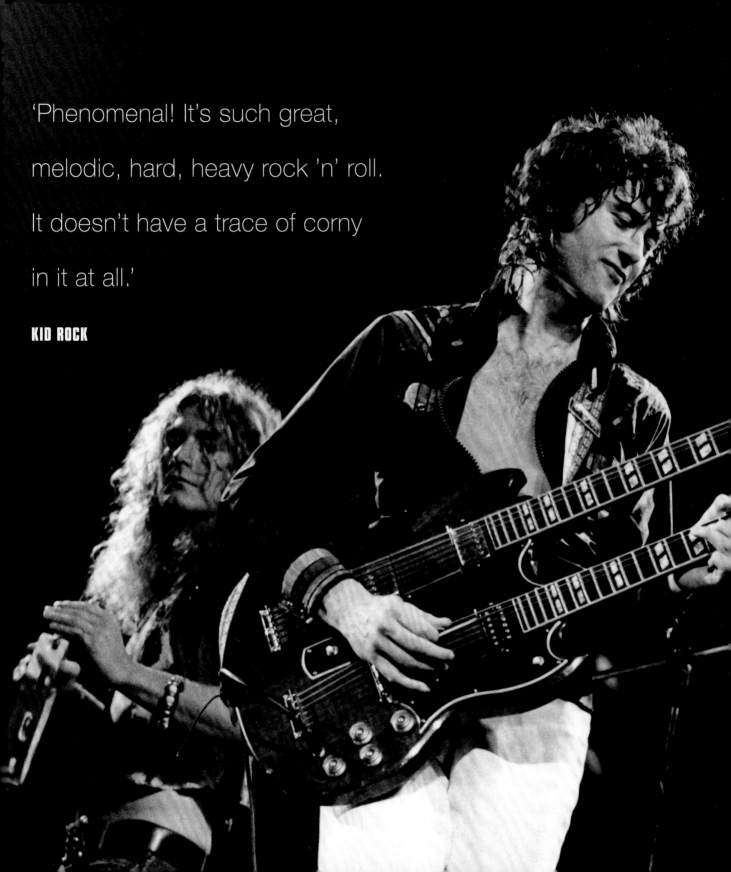

'Phenomenal! It's such great, melodic, hard, heavy rock 'n' roll. It doesn't have a trace of corny in it at all.'

KID ROCK

broke the record for the number of tickets sold at a venue to see a single act. Four years later they broke their own record. And, crucially, they got to keep more of the money they generated than any of their rivals.

They changed the music of the 1970s, creating heavy metal, which became the dominant musical style of the decade. And they changed the music business for ever. Every successful band since Led Zeppelin has reaped the benefits of their power.

In the end their power sowed the seeds of their own destruction, as they proved the old adage 'Absolute power corrupts absolutely'. Although what actually brought them down was the death of their drummer, a blow from which they could not recover. But at the height of their power – during the first half of the 1970s – they were the biggest rock band the world had ever seen.

'I'm the world's biggest Led Zeppelin fan. The music, the way they conducted themselves, their whole management structure – they were the blueprint. Queen always used to play "The Immigrant Song" in sound-checks just for the glory of the sound.'

BRIAN MAY

Whole Lotta Success

The power of Led Zeppelin's music was so great because, as a band, they understood the importance of dynamics. By combining brute force with subtlety, they gave their music a drama that set them apart from their rivals.

'Jimmy Page stands alone as a conceptualizer of what a rock band should sound like. And the greatness of Zeppelin comes from him as a writer and a producer.'

RITCHIE BLACKMORE

Power on Record

As professional musicians, Jimmy Page and John Paul Jones applied their knowledge and technique in the studio to achieve the dramatic effects they were looking for. Robert Plant and John Bonham initially relied more on instinct, although it was no less effective. As experienced session musicians, Page and Jones knew how to put their drama on record. On their first album the drama is achieved in somewhat rudimentary fashion – not surprisingly, as they had known each other for less than a month.

'Led Zeppelin had a heavy influence on Rush in our early days. Page's loose style of playing showed an immense confidence, and there are no rules to his playing.' ALEX LIFESON

The second album, recorded in haste at different studios in America and Britain as the band toured relentlessly to build their reputation, shows signs that Page was beginning to understand the band chemistry that he had at his disposal. By the third album, Page and Plant had struck up the songwriting partnership – after sequestering themselves in the remote Welsh cottage of Bron-Yr-Aur – that would shape the band's music.

But it wasn't until the fourth album, often referred to as the *Four Symbols*, that all the elements of the band seemed to fall into place and they nailed the musical style with which they would always be associated. Subsequent albums emphasized different elements of their style, as they stretched out and experimented without losing the core sensibility that bound them together.

Power on Stage

Led Zeppelin's onstage chemistry was obvious to everyone who watched them at their earliest shows. Indeed, one of the abiding memories of those who saw them as they relentlessly gigged their way towards headline status was of the band members exchanging incredulous looks, unable to believe how good they were together.

Within four years, Led Zeppelin had become the dominant force in rock'n'roll. And it was as a live band with shows that regularly lasted three hours that Led Zeppelin wielded their sovereignty. Bonham's drums were described by Page as sounding 'like cannons'. Page himself had only to don the twin-necked Gibson guitar that signalled 'Stairway to Heaven' for the stadium to erupt in joyous anticipation. Plant would flex his rock-god limbs, barely encased by his skinny blouses and tight jeans, and in the shadows Jones would pummel away on his bass, occasionally putting it aside to add swathes of synthesizer.

Sadly, Led Zeppelin's prowess as a live band was not appreciated by those who didn't see them perform during their lifetime. Their concert film, *The Song Remains the Same*, failed to do them justice, crippled by self-conscious over-production. It was not until 1997, when *BBC Sessions* was released containing two live concerts from 1969 and 1971, that the band's majestic stage presence was revealed. *Led Zeppelin DVD* in 2003 roamed across the band's career adding the visual impact, while *How the West Was Won* later the same year caught the band's two-and-a-half-hour show from 1972, when Page believes they were at their height.

1960-67: What They Did First

T he origins of Led Zeppelin lie in the London session musician scene and the Birmingham rock scene. But if Jimmy Page was the only 'known' musician among them, the other three had all paid their dues. Indeed, they were still paying them right up to the moment they gathered together and started rehearsing their first album.

'Little' Jimmy Page

Jimmy Page (b. 1944) grew up in Heston, West London, and started strumming an acoustic guitar aged 12, forming a skiffle group that made a brief TV appearance on a talent show the following year. He left school at 16, joining Neil Christian & The Crusaders as a guitarist but quickly graduated to the London session scene, becoming one of the most in-demand players due to his ability to play almost any style. He appeared on literally hundreds of records between 1962 and 1968, most

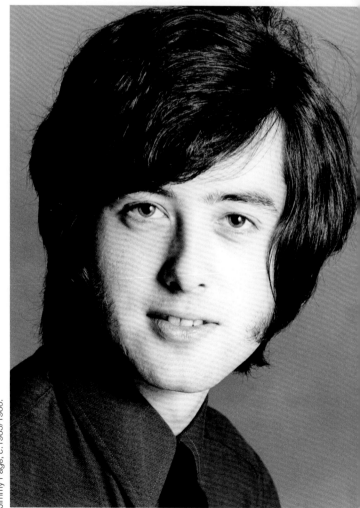

Jimmy Page, c.1965/1966.

notably on Joe Cocker's 'With a Little Help From My Friends'. He was known as 'Little' Jimmy Page to distinguish him from the other leading session guitarist, 'Big' Jim Sullivan.

John Paul Jones

On his travels around the London studios, Page would regularly come into contact with John Paul Jones (b. John Baldwin, 1946), a noted session bass player and musical arranger, who had grown up in a musical family in Sidcup, South London, before joining ex-Shadows Jet Harris and Tony Meehan in

'The first time I saw Led Zeppelin … we just couldn't believe the power and the sound. People are still today trying to imitate Led Zeppelin.' ROGER TAYLOR

1962. Two years later, he moved into the session scene and soon became a go-to musician and arranger for Decca Records, hit producer Mickie Most (Donovan, Herman's Hermits, Lulu) and Andrew Loog Oldham's Immediate label, where Jimmy Page was also an in-house producer.

Robert Plant

Born in 1948, Robert Plant grew up in Kidderminster just outside Birmingham and after leaving grammar school at the age of 16 and the family home shortly afterwards, he started singing with various bands on the West Midlands blues circuit. In 1967, he got a solo deal with CBS Records and released a couple of unsuccessful singles. Afterwards he returned to the Midlands and resumed gigging with local bands that included the Crawling King Snakes – which was where he met John Bonham.

John Bonham

Born in Redditch, Worcestershire, in 1948, John Bonham was fashioning homemade drum kits out of household appliances before he was in his teens. He got his first proper kit shortly

Band of Joy, 1968. Robert Plant, second from left; John Bonham, centre.

before he left school and started playing with local bands, supplementing his meagre earnings by working at his father's building company. His aggressive, sometimes violent style brought him into conflict with some venue managers, who banned him from their premises. But musicians were in awe of his forceful beat, none more so than Robert Plant when he encountered him in the Crawling King Snakes.

The Band of Joy

Both Plant and Bonham were just 'passing through' the Crawling King Snakes. Plant left in 1967 to join the fledgling Band of Joy, whose blend of blues and soul was drawing a

'Led Zeppelin was an affair of the heart. Each of the members was important to the sum total of what we were.' JIMMY PAGE

mod audience. However, he left due to management issues and attempted, unsuccessfully, to form his own Band of Joy. He was more successful with a third incarnation of the band that included Bonham, and the band expanded its touring boundaries as far as London. In early 1968, they recorded a number of demos, but failed to get a record contract and broke up soon afterwards.

Jimmy Page Joins The Yardbirds

Jimmy Page was first asked to join the Yardbirds in 1965, replacing Eric Clapton. But he turned them down, correctly figuring that the session scene was more lucrative. When

'I know when I wear a Led Zeppelin t-shirt, I am happy to put that Led Zeppelin t-shirt on. It's not, "Well, they kind of suck".' NIKKI SIXX

'The first time I heard Led Zeppelin, I had to pull over. One of a kind and a complete mystique, an enigma and probably one of the heaviest bands of all time.' RICHIE SAMBORA

he was asked again a year later, the session world had lost some of its allure and he accepted, despite the fact that his role involved playing bass behind Jeff Beck. That all changed when Beck started missing gigs during an American tour and Page filled in, eventually landing the job full time.

But by early 1968, the Yardbirds were sinking. They were flat broke after four years of relentless touring and recording. Their management was remote and it was only when the burly Peter Grant came on board that they began to see any money. Page was particularly impressed by his constant close attention to the group. For the others, it was too late.

1968: The New Yardbirds

When the Yardbirds broke up in the summer of 1968, Jimmy Page and Peter Grant were already making plans for a new group, musically based on the Jeff Beck Group's first album, *Truth*, and using the marketing template of Cream, who had achieved unprecedented success in America. Page and Jones had already agreed that they would collaborate in a new venture.

'We played for hours and we only had an hour-and-a-half set. So if anyone knew more than four bars of any tune we would go into it.' JOHN PAUL JONES

A New Band Emerges

For a singer they approached the mercurial but idiosyncratic Terry Reid, who turned them down but recommended they check out Plant. So Page and Grant travelled up to Birmingham to see him playing with Hobbstweedle, his latest band. Page was convinced after just one listen and after a few days at Page's house in Pangbourne, Berkshire, Plant agreed to join. Plant also recommended Bonham as a drummer. He was touring with singer-songwriter Tim Rose and when they tracked him down they discovered that Joe Cocker and Chris Farlowe were also interested in his services. It took some persuasion and around 40 telegrams to his house (which didn't have a telephone) to win him over.

'Fox News will one day come to an end. Led Zeppelin will not. It's as simple as that.'

HENRY ROLLINS

The New Yardbirds Tour Scandinavia

With the line-up now in place, the band worked up a set of new songs and R&B numbers before heading out on a 10-day tour of Scandinavia that had been booked for the Yardbirds. They billed themselves as the New Yardbirds and quickly worked themselves into a tight musical unit. By the time of their first US tour, they were joined by Richard Cole who had been a roadie with the Yardbirds and was now hired by Peter Grant as the band's road manager. The pair of them formed a tight protective cordon around the band.

Led Zeppelin Is Born

There are several versions of how the band came to be known as Led Zeppelin and most of them involve Keith Moon and/or John Entwistle of The Who, who were disillusioned with their own band at that time and were considering forming a breakaway group. Entwistle claims that he came up with the name Lead Zeppelin; Page says that Moon suggested it to him as it seemed to fit the music they were playing. It was Grant who shortened the first word, as he felt that Americans might mispronounce it. Another version is that Page was

impressed by the name Iron Butterfly, an American group he'd supported with the Yardbirds, and was on the lookout for something similar.

Recording the First Album

Returning from Scandinavia, the group booked time at London Olympic Studios and recorded their debut album in a total of 36 hours during October. Page's production

'Back in the old days, we were often compared to Led Zeppelin. If we did something with harmony, it was the Beach Boys. Something heavy was Led Zeppelin.'

FREDDIE MERCURY

'The group was very loud.
It might have been all right
for one of those massive
American stadiums but it was
overpoweringly loud for the
Marquee.' JOHN GEE (MARQUEE MANAGER)

Ahmet Ertegun, co-founder of Atlantic Records.

caught the raw power and unabashed confidence they'd already developed playing live. Seven of the nine songs were credited to Page and other group members (but not Plant, who was having issues with his publishing company).

In between recording sessions they fulfilled a couple more shows as the New Yardbirds and played their first gig under their own name at Surrey University. They made their London debut at the Roundhouse on 9 November 1968, the same day Plant married his heavily pregnant girlfriend Maureen.

Signing to Atlantic Records in New York

When the album was completed, Grant took the finished tapes to New York and met with Atlantic Records, the label that had signed Cream in America. He played them the album, explained that the band would be focusing their efforts on the American market and offered them worldwide rights. In turn he demanded complete creative control over the band's records and artwork. The deal was agreed at once, with Atlantic paying an unprecedented $200,000 advance. This gave the band financial security when they started touring.

1969: Led Zeppelin Unleashed

At the beginning of 1969, Led Zeppelin were complete unknowns. By the end of that year, they were all-conquering rock'n'roll heroes with a reputation for on- and offstage excess that would become the stuff of legend. During the year, they released two platinum albums and were already working on a third. They also played four American tours, three as headliners.

First American Tour

Led Zeppelin played their first American show at Denver, Colorado on Boxing Day 1968 after warm-up shows in Britain. After supporting Vanilla Fudge and the MC5 at the Boston Tea Party they started 1969 supporting Country Joe & The Fish for three nights at San Francisco's Fillmore West. The plan was to reach as many people as possible and, cushioned by their large record company advance, the fee

The Americans had it their own way for so long. As soon as some competition comes along, the not-so-good American bands get uptight because they think they're missing out on all the work.' JOHN PAUL JONES

was largely irrelevant. Once on stage, the band's shock-and-awe style with its raw dynamics from Page's guitar, Plant's orgasmic vocals and Bonham's thunderous drums never failed.

Led Zeppelin I

Their debut album, *Led Zeppelin I*, released in mid-January in the US, got mixed reviews and gathered pace gradually, peaking at No. 10 but staying in the charts for 16 months. Returning to the UK in March, they played a club tour to coincide with the album's UK release, along with a radio session and a TV appearance. The album peaked at No. 6, staying in the charts for five months.

Second American Tour

Back in the US in late April, Led Zeppelin embarked on their second tour, this time as headliners because most groups were now reluctant to follow their barnstorming set that already ran to two hours. It was noticeable that they were attracting a younger audience, who had missed out on The Beatles and the Rolling Stones but now had their own rock'n'roll heroes to worship, and did so with exuberance.

This was the tour that gave Led Zeppelin their reputation for hedonism and debauchery. At the Hyatt House Hotel in

'I realized what Led Zeppelin was about around the end of our first US tour. We started off not even on the bill in Denver, and by the time we got to New York we were second to Iron Butterfly, and they didn't want to go on!'

ROBERT PLANT

'When I was little and I was introduced to Led Zeppelin, I didn't know what a Zeppelin was or who Led Zeppelin was. The real meaning is whatever feelings and memories you attach to the music.' **KYP MALONE**

Los Angeles – subsequently nicknamed the Riot House – Page was wheeled into a room full of eager groupies on a room-service trolley. And then there was 'The Infamous Mud Shark Incident' at the Edgewater Inn in Seattle. Amid the mayhem the band were working on their second album, writing songs in hotel rooms and recording at different studios along the way.

They found their UK popularity catching up when they returned in June for a series of shows, including their biggest show yet at the Bath Festival and another at London's Royal Albert Hall, where they carried on playing after the house lights had been turned on.

Third American Tour

Arriving back in the States in early July, Led Zeppelin played a series of summer festivals across the country and were now starting to make serious money as a live act, having lost money on their first tour. At the Singer Bowl in Flushing Meadows, an inebriated Bonham nearly got himself arrested when he joined in the all-star jam at the end and played the beat to 'The Stripper' while removing his clothes. Fortunately Grant reached him just ahead

of the police and carried him offstage, locking him in a dressing room.

Fourth American Tour

Warming up with a show at London's Lyceum Ballroom (which had been damaged by a German Zeppelin 50 years earlier), Led Zeppelin flew back to America in October for a prestigious date at New York's Carnegie Hall before embarking on a three-week tour.

Led Zeppelin II

Led Zeppelin II was released in the US in mid-October with advance orders of 400,000. It raced to No. 2, where it stayed behind The Beatles' Abbey Road, eventually taking over the No. 1 spot in late December, where it stayed for seven weeks. When Atlantic Records discovered that radio stations were making their own edits to 'Whole Lotta Love', they released their own version that reached No. 4. But the band were not amused and refused to release any singles in the UK, where the album spent just one week at No. 1 but stayed in the charts for an astonishing two-and-a-half years.

'Right from the first time we went to America in 1968, Led Zeppelin was a word-of-mouth thing. You can't really compare it to how it is today.'

JIMMY PAGE

1970: On a Stairway to Heaven

After a year blitzing America with frantic abandon, Led Zeppelin began 1970 by taking Britain and Europe by the scruff of the neck.

Taking the UK by Strategy

Led Zeppelin II topped the British charts in the last week of 1969. A week later, the band started a tour of British town halls, playing without a support, so they could indulge their two-hour set without breaking curfew regulations. By now, Jones had a Hammond organ onstage for some songs. There was a minor scare when Plant was involved in a car crash driving back from a Spirit gig (particularly for Page who was woken in the middle of the night at home by the police).

There were problems at the start of a European tour, notably when Eva von Zeppelin showed up in Denmark to accuse them of besmirching the family name. For a couple

John Bonham with Peter Grant, right.

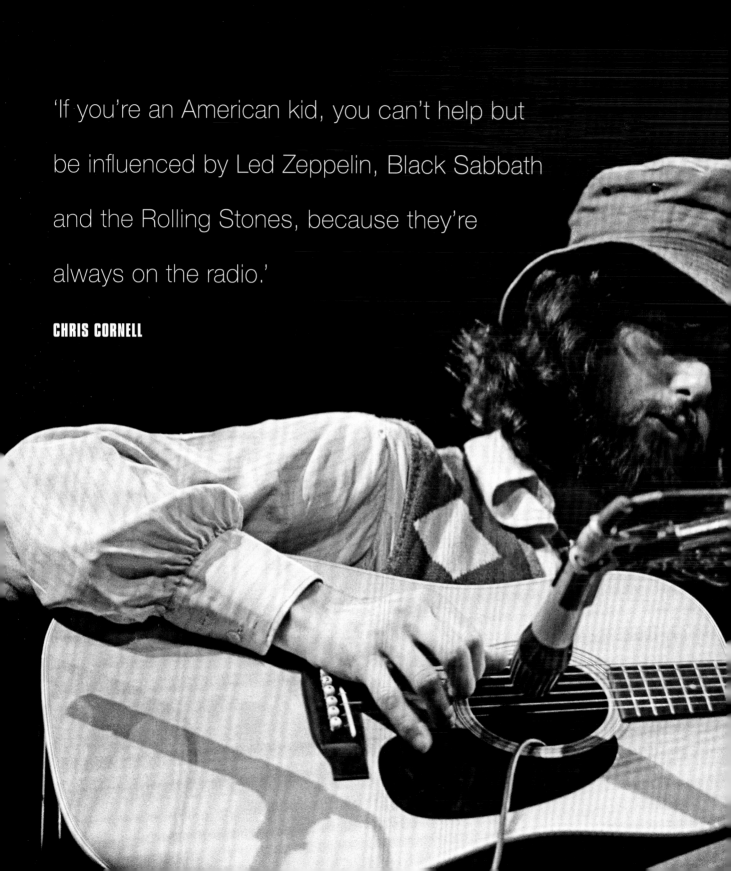

'If you're an American kid, you can't help but be influenced by Led Zeppelin, Black Sabbath and the Rolling Stones, because they're always on the radio.'

CHRIS CORNELL

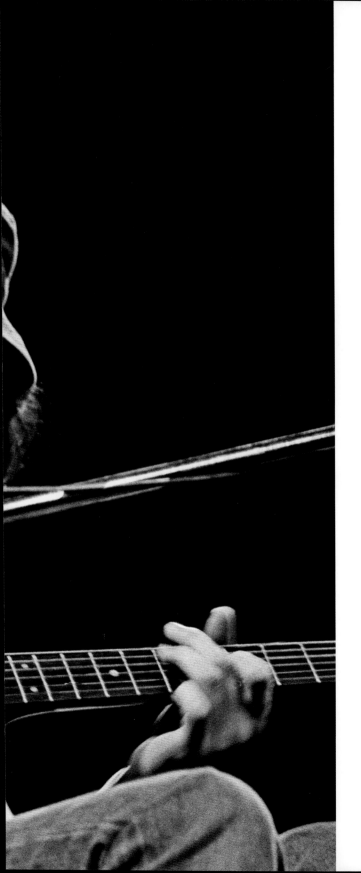

of gigs they were billed as The Nobs. Meanwhile, Page had become increasingly fascinated by Aleister Crowley, who had dedicated his life to exploring the darker side of the human soul, and bought Crowley's run-down and allegedly haunted residence, Boleskine House, on the shores of Loch Ness in Scotland.

'Music was so important to the culture when I was growing up in the Sixties and Seventies. […] It was like, "Okay, here's another great record by Bob Dylan; here's another great record by Led Zeppelin."

JOHN MELLENCAMP

'They may be world famous but a couple of shrieking monkeys are not going to use a privileged family name without permission.'

EVA VON ZEPPELIN

Back in the US in March, they encountered a darker mood as protests against the Vietnam War increased and their shows were frequently ringed by riot police looking for an excuse to move in. In response they beefed up their own security, but it meant their own freedoms were curtailed and, like their audiences, they unleashed their pent-up energies at the shows – which only served to rack up the tensions still higher.

Bron-Yr-Aur

Fortunately the band were back in Britain by the time things turned really ugly in America with the shootings at Ohio's Kent State University in May. While Jones and Bonham relaxed with their families, Page and Plant retreated to idyllic seclusion at the Bron-Yr-Aur cottage in Snowdonia, North Wales, to work up songs for the next album. There was a stripped-down, acoustic flavour to many of the songs that were put together by an open fire after long walks in the country.

They emerged in public again in late June, in front of 150,000 fans at the climax to the three-day Bath Festival. Opening with the barnstorming, newly written

'Immigrant Song', their masterful performance confirmed that they were the biggest band in the world after the Rolling Stones. Then it was back to business in America once more.

Their coronation took place at the annual *Melody Maker* Poll Awards, held at London's Savoy Hotel in September, where they were voted 'Best Band', displacing The Beatles who had won it for the previous eight years. *Led Zeppelin II* was 'Best Album' and Plant was 'Best Male Vocalist'. It was an astonishing achievement for a band that had come third in the 'Best Newcomer' category the previous year and Page, Plant and Bonham interrupted their sixth US tour to fly back and soak up the accolades.

Led Zeppelin III

After their UK triumph, the release of *Led Zeppelin III* in October brought them back to Earth with a jolt. It wasn't just the critics who took issue with the gentle acoustic numbers that took up much of the album; the fans seemed to agree. Although the album shot to No. 1 in the US and UK, it started falling down the charts more quickly than its predecessor.

Page was stung. When they got back to England, he and Plant returned to Bron-Yr-Aur and they started to put some flesh on the bones of an idea that Page had been carrying around for a while. As they worked around Page's chord sequence it was clear that they were on to something. The eight-minute song that emerged would be their defining masterpiece – 'Stairway to Heaven'.

'There's so much music from Led Zeppelin that I think I overlooked when I was a kid because I didn't understand it, so now to revisit it at an older age, I have a deeper appreciation for it.'

BRENDON URIE

1971: The Biggest Band in the World

D etermined to make up for the relative failure of *Led Zeppelin III*, the band spent the first two months of 1971 recording their next album before heading out on a UK tour, revisiting venues they had struggled to fill two years earlier.

Knuckling Down

With 'Stairway to Heaven' waiting for its chance to shine in the studio, Led Zeppelin decamped to Headley Grange, an empty manor house in Hampshire, in January to work on the basic tracks for their next album. These included the opening double whammy of 'Black Dog' and 'Rock and Roll' that would give the lie to anyone claiming the band had gone soft. The album took shape in February back at London's Island and Olympic studios with Sandy Denny, Fairport Convention's singer and winner of *Melody Maker*'s 'Best Female Vocalist' in 1970, providing a superb foil for

John Paul Jones, Hiroshima, Japan, 1971.

Plant's wailing on 'The Battle of Evermore'. All that remained was to mix the album.

With a sigh of relief, the band embarked on a British tour in March, playing many of the same venues they had played just two years earlier, including London's Marquee Club. They charged the same price as before and had no trouble filling any of the venues. The band had a blast, but they left crowds of disappointed, ticketless fans hanging around outside everywhere they went.

'When I was young, a gatefold album by Pink Floyd or Led Zeppelin was something to get excited about, something you longed for.'

MARK KOZELEK

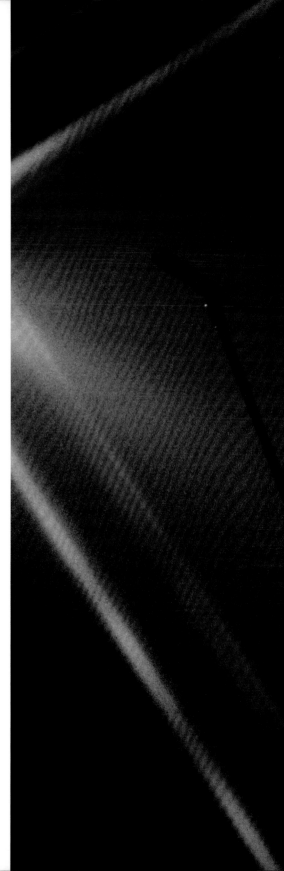

A Real Mix-Up

Page went out to Los Angeles to supervise the album mix at Sunset Studios. But when he returned and played the results to the others, it sounded nothing like he had been hearing in LA. Something, somewhere, had gone wrong. There was no alternative but to go back to the original tapes and start the mixing process again.

'The first song I played all the way through must have been "Stairway to Heaven". I remember getting through the fingerpicking and just cursing Jimmy Page.'

JOHNNY DEPP

It also meant that they had to start their seventh American tour in August without a new album to promote. The 20 dates that had been set up across the country would earn the band a million dollars. They did not disappoint and, after a break in Hawaii, they made their first visit to Japan where they played five shows. The shows were ecstatically received, although they narrowly avoided a crisis when Jones was taken ill before one show and Atlantic Records' executive Phil Carson had to deputize at short notice. The Japanese were less impressed by the band's riotous antics between shows, however, and they found themselves banned from the Tokyo Hilton.

Led Zeppelin IV

The fourth Led Zeppelin album was finally released in early November, although it was hard to know what to call it. There was no title and no sign of the band's name. There was no mention of the band members apart from 'produced by Jimmy Page' on the record label. There were, however, four symbols representing each member of the band that were printed on the cover spine. The cover itself featured a rustic gentleman bent down under the weight of a bundle of sticks on a peeling wall that was cut away on the back cover to reveal a crumbling housing estate with a modern tower block in the distance. Inside, the gatefold sleeve had a drawing of an occult-like hermit standing over a rocky cliff face. While the cover images sparked speculation that continues to this day, the music brooked no argument: the album remains Led Zeppelin's finest achievement.

However, the album failed to top the American charts, being held at bay by *Santana III* and Sly and the Family Stone's *There's a Riot Going On*, although it stayed in the charts for nearly six months. In the UK it got to No. 1 and was still in the charts 14 months later. Led Zeppelin ended the year with another British tour, this time at larger venues to accommodate their following, and included two nights at Wembley Empire Pool where they delivered a three-hour set, their reputation restored.

'They played just about everything they've ever written. Nothing, just nothing, was spared. ... So they get paid a lot of bread. Well, people paid that bread, and I reckon they got every penny's worth.'

ROY HOLLINGWORTH, MELODY MAKER

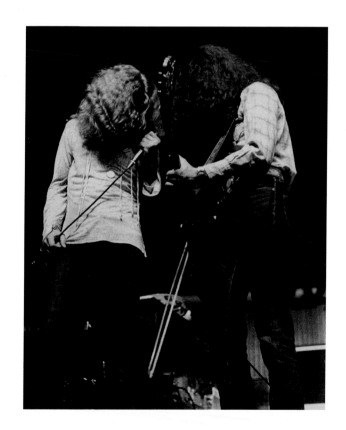

'I saw Deep Purple live once and I paid money for it and I thought, "Geez, this is ridiculous." I never liked those Deep Purples [...]. I always thought it was a poor man's Led Zeppelin.'

ANGUS YOUNG

1972: Ripping up the Rule Book

Keen to expand their touring horizons, Led Zeppelin played their first Australasian tour in 1972, receiving the same rapturous reception they were getting everywhere else. They spent a couple of months rehearsing and recording their next album (which wouldn't be released until the following year) before getting back to the business of touring – America, Japan and Britain. And those fans…

'If you listen to our work, from *Led Zeppelin I* to *Coda*, it's just a fantastic textbook.'

JIMMY PAGE

Jimmy Page

Robert Plant

John Bonham

LED ZEPPELIN

John Paul Jones

Going Down Under

When Page met up with fellow Aleister Crowley fan, film director Kenneth Anger, and discovered he was making a film about Satanism and the occult titled *Lucifer Rising*, it seemed like a match made in Heaven (or Hell). Page agreed to provide the soundtrack to the film and worked on it whenever his busy Led Zeppelin schedule permitted. But the relationship soured when, after three years, Page had only come up with 20 minutes of music that Anger felt was unusable.

In February, Led Zeppelin embarked on their first Australasian tour. They were supposed to play a show in Singapore en route but the authorities refused them entry because of their long hair. In fact they wouldn't even let them off the plane. The Australians were more welcoming and the eight shows included two open-air concerts in Sydney, Australia and Auckland, New Zealand, each attended by around 25,000 fans.

On the way back, Page and Plant stopped off in India to explore the local musical culture and began thinking of ways in which the Eastern and Western musical forms could be blended together.

'The days of the promoter giving a few quid to the band ... against the money taken at the door are gone. The business was run by managers, agents and promoters when it is the groups who bring the people in.' PETER GRANT

Holy Houses

Back in Britain, the band installed themselves at Mick Jagger's country home at Stargroves, Hampshire, and started working up ideas for their next album, which they recorded on to the Rolling Stones' mobile studio. Unlike their previous albums, there was no fixed plan for the next. The band was more open to trying out different ideas. Page had various experimental chord sequences he'd been working on at his home studio and Jones was keen to expand his keyboard role.

In May, they switched to London's Olympic Studio, where the album began to take shape. The first fruits of their foray into Eastern music could be heard on 'The Song Remains the Same' and there were also a couple of uncharacteristic tracks – the reggae-ish 'D'yer Mak'er' and the funky 'The Crunge'. The overdubbing and mixing sessions took place at New York's Electric Ladyland while the band prepared for their eighth US tour.

Getting Their Dues

Led Zeppelin tightened their grip on the American touring business for their summer tour. Such was the band's drawing power that they were now able to demand 90 per cent of the gate money, leaving the promoter to make his profit on the remaining 10 per cent. It was another groundbreaking move by Grant, who fought tenaciously to get the best possible deals for his band.

The Rolling Stones were also touring America that summer and it irked Led Zeppelin that, although they were out-performing the Stones in many areas, it was the Stones who were getting all the media coverage. So they hired a leading public relations company to improve their image.

Ladies of the Road

Zeppelin had always been suspicious of the media and they certainly didn't want the media reporting on some of their riotous antics on tour, particularly when they got to the West Coast and installed themselves at the Los Angeles Hyatt House, or 'Riot House' as it had become known. Page was openly cavorting with Pamela Des Barres, the queen of the notorious LA groupie scene, but when he was introduced to 14-year-old, doe-eyed Lori Maddox, he was instantly smitten. And when Bebe Buell arrived on the scene later, the soap opera knew no bounds.

After an autumn break during which Page bought an eighteenth-century manor house in Plumpton, Sussex, Led Zeppelin were back in Japan in October for their second tour and then embarked on their biggest ever UK tour that would stretch into the following year – as would the release of their fifth album, which was beset by cover problems.

'It [John Paul Jones] was feeling the frustrations of the goldfish-bowl life, he'd take a television set to pieces and glue it upside down on the ceiling in the correct order.' ROBERT PLANT

1973-74: Rock Royalty

Houses of the Holy was released in March and the band spent the first seven months of the year touring. But the stress of constant touring was starting to take its toll, particularly on Bonham, despite the band making use of a private plane.

Houses of the Holy

The printers finally got the colours right on Led Zeppelin's fifth album, which was released in March while the band were touring Europe. It was the first to have a title, *Houses of the Holy*, a reference to the venues where the band communed with their audiences. The album had a more relaxed feel to it than its predecessors and the critics were divided by its diversity. Some were upset by a seeming lack of direction, others praised the band for broadening out, but nothing the critics or anyone else had to say stopped the album from getting to No. 1 around the world.

'I think Led Zeppelin must
have worn some of the most
peculiar clothing that men
had ever been seen to wear
without cracking a smile.'

ROBERT PLANT

As soon as the European dates were finished, the band began preparing for their next American tour, which would be the biggest production they had put together so far in terms of lighting and sound, and required some 30 technicians to ensure that it ran smoothly.

On Tour With 'The Beast'

The three-month US tour started in early May with the band staying in selected bases around the country and chartering their own plane to fly them to and from the shows. But

the incessant touring was starting to take its toll on the band members. Plant was prone to flu and had to take particular care of his voice from air conditioning and varying temperatures. Page found that the different time zones and touring lifestyle played havoc with his eating and sleeping habits and he sometimes looked alarmingly trall. Bonham reacted badly to being away from his wife and family and was prone to destructive rages, particularly when drunk, which was much of the time. His nickname had switched from the avuncular 'Bonzo' to 'The Beast' and not without reason.

Along the way the band broke The Beatles' eight-year-old record for the biggest audience for a single group show, when they drew 56,000 fans to the Tampa Stadium in Florida. Their three New York shows at Madison Square Gardens in July were filmed for a movie that would eventually come out as *The Song Remains the Same*. But before the final show, tour manager Richard Cole discovered that $200,000 that had been put in a safe deposit box at their hotel had gone missing. The FBI was called in but the money was never recovered. By way of compensation, the tour grossed $4.5 million. The band flew home in August to recover and film individual sequences for the movie in the autumn, including manager Peter Grant. But it would take another three years before it was released.

The Birth of Swan Song

The band took a much-needed break from touring in 1974, instead spending time recording their next album, which would turn out to be a double. They also launched their own record label, Swan Song Records, which was intended not just for their own record releases but for other bands as well. The label was launched with a press conference in London followed by two big parties in New York and Los Angeles.

'I love The Beatles and when I was very young, I had young parents, so Led Zeppelin and Janis Joplin and Jimi Hendrix and The Beatles constantly were big influences on my life.' PHIL ANSELMO

John Paul Jones plays organ on the band's private jet, 'The Starship' during US tour, 1973.

Their first signing, the newly formed Bad Company, featuring former Free vocalist Paul Rodgers, got off to a phenomenal start when their self-titled debut album topped the American charts. Other signings included Maggie Bell and the Pretty Things, whose new album was launched with a spectacular – and debauched – Hallowe'en party in Chislehurst Caves. Between their recording sessions, the band members occasionally took time out to play with friends and label-mates, but mainly they kept a low profile. Even Bonham stayed out of trouble, except when Mott the Hoople unwisely declined his offer to jam with them in New York and a drunken backstage fracas ensued.

'If you look at the guys in the Seventies, like Led Zeppelin, they had bigger planes than we do, they had more money. But they weren't singing about it.' **LENNY KRAVITZ**

1975: Exiled in America

A fter a year off the road, Led Zeppelin returned with a major US tour at the start of 1975 that was hampered by injuries and illnesses as well as rioting fans.

Physical Damage and Physical Graffiti

Led Zeppelin intended to roar out of the blocks with a major American tour that required a 44-strong road crew and now came with a laser show. But they were beset by mishaps: Page broke a finger in a train-carriage door which meant that some songs had to be dropped from the band's set while it healed; Plant's flu hampered several shows; fans rioting for tickets in Boston caused the show to be cancelled; and the constant threat of a one-man riot from Bonham created an undercurrent of tension.

'I didn't really get to Led Zeppelin until I was in my twenties.' ANTHONY KIEDIS

But the atmosphere lightened considerably with the release of *Physical Graffiti*, a double album that was driven by the anthemic, Eastern-influenced 'Kashmir', the heavy, metallic 'Trampled Underfoot' and the intense 11-minute blues-rock blitz of 'In My Time of Dying'. For the first time, a Led Zeppelin album was greeted with almost universal acclaim and it spent six weeks at the top of the US charts.

Triumph at Earl's Court

The band returned to Britain in April and the following month played a five-night series of shows at London's Earl's Court. It was the first time British fans had had the chance to appreciate the full scale of the band's American presentation, to which video screens had now been added. They also included an acoustic section in the show that the intensity of their American shows did not permit.

'I believe that the Rolling Stones and Led Zeppelin are two of the greatest rock bands ever!'

JESSE VENTURA

Afterwards, the band left the country and set up base in Montreux, Switzerland, as they planned to spend a year away from the UK to reduce what they regarded as a crippling tax burden. Tours of North and South America were being lined up for the autumn, but in the meantime the band relaxed into a life of exile. Page and Plant took off on a motoring holiday to Morocco, leaving civilization behind as they drove deep into the Sahara Desert. The music they encountered along the way set them thinking about more new musical directions.

Plant's Catastrophic Car Crash

The band's leisurely idyll was shattered in early August. Plant, on holiday with his family in Rhodes, was badly injured when their car careered off the road. He suffered multiple fractures to his ankle and elbow, while his wife fractured her skull and pelvis. They were taken to hospital in the back of a passing fruit truck and frantic efforts then ensued to get them airlifted back to Britain.

Even then their problems were not over. Plant had already used up his 'tax-free' allocation of days in the UK and so, encased in plaster, he was rushed to Heathrow Airport, where he was hoisted on board an aeroplane by a fork-lift truck and flown to Jersey in the Channel Islands. All plans for the band were cancelled.

Recovery and Recording

Plant remained in Jersey, beginning his slow recovery and was visited by London specialists who monitored his progress. For a while, he was forbidden to stand or put any pressure on his broken ankle, as doctors warned he might never walk again. Once his condition improved a little, he flew to California where he was installed in a beach house in Malibu.

'I just picked up a lot of classic-rock, melodic influence from my mom, music that she listened to, like 10,000 Maniacs, Led Zeppelin, REO Speedwagon and Yes.' YELAWOLF

Page came out to visit him and to combat the boredom they started working on ideas for a new album. Soon they were joined by Jones and Bonham for some serious rehearsals. In November, they all decamped to Munich, Germany, where they recorded the album in less than three weeks. They returned to Jersey to spend Christmas as close to the UK as possible and played an unannounced show at a local dancehall. On New Year's Eve, Plant finally walked unaided again.

'Our intent with Led Zeppelin was not to get caught up in the singles market, but to make albums where you could really flex your muscles – your musical intellect, if you like – and challenge yourself.'

JIMMY PAGE

1976: Dazed and Confused

With Led Zeppelin's tax exile set to continue until May and Plant recovering gradually from his car crash injuries, the band fretted impatiently.

Presence

Not a band used to hanging around with nothing to do, Led Zeppelin spent the first part of the year fidgeting in New York and bemoaning their nomadic exile to anyone who would listen. Page meanwhile busied himself mixing and preparing the soundtrack to the band's upcoming live concert movie.

Premiere of *The Song Remains The Same*, Fox Wilshire theater, LA, 1976.

'Dad told me that before I was born, he would put my mom's stomach up to the speaker and play Led Zeppelin.'

THOMAS RHETT

Their inevitably delayed (by the cover yet again) seventh album, *Presence*, was finally released in April and seemed to reflect the band's schizophrenic mood. Aside from the monumental 10-minute opening 'Achilles Last Stand', an unrelenting, controlled thrash into which every band member seemed to have channelled all his frustrations, and the swirling, atmospheric 'Nobody's Fault But Mine', the rest of the album seemed curiously listless. But the advance orders were enough to send it straight to No. 1 in the US with instant platinum status, although it failed to rise above No. 2 in the UK.

'I wanted to be a composer before anything else.
And my sister was listening to Led Zeppelin in the other room! When I heard that, it was a game changer.'

STEVE VAI

Summer of Discontent

In May, the band returned to Britain and their families. But Page soon found himself in a public spat with film director Kenneth Anger over the music he'd been writing for his *Lucifer Rising* film. He and Bonham then travelled to Switzerland to record a percussion piece that Bonham had been working on. Afterwards, Bonham spent some time in the South of France with his family, but when they returned home he moved on to Monte Carlo. There he nearly got himself into serious trouble at a nightclub packed with wealthy patrons and their bodyguards, when he pistol-whipped his roadie in a drunken rage and had to be restrained at the cost of a broken nose before the club erupted into violence. It was the latest of several drunken incidents, often involving violence, that Bonham had instigated in clubs, gigs and even aeroplanes in recent months and there were growing concerns for his mental welfare among the band's management.

The Song Remains the Same

In October, the Led Zeppelin concert movie, *The Song Remains the Same*, was premiered in New York, where the shows had been filmed three years earlier. The concert

'Led Zeppelin was a band that would change things around substantially each time we played.... We were becoming tighter and tighter, to the point of telepathy.' **JIMMY PAGE**

footage was spliced with shots of the band members at home with their families and fantasy sequences devised by each of them. While the film caught the spectacular flavour of a Led Zeppelin concert, the shows themselves, coming at the end of a gruelling tour, were not among the band's most inspired. It was clear that the band were aware of being filmed and this may have hampered their musical performance. Some of the fantasy sequences distracted from the music and the fictional scenes of gratuitous violence depicted by manager Peter Grant and tour manager Richard Cole were viewed by some as inappropriate given their reputation for bullying and intimidation. Although the film did pick up some awards and grossed over $200,000 in its

first week in America, it was perhaps telling that Grant described it as 'the most expensive home movie ever made'.

The accompanying soundtrack, which contained songs not featured in the movie and vice versa, also emphasized the band's increasingly indulgent approach, in particular on 'Dazed and Confused', which ran to nearly 27 minutes. Nevertheless, the album topped the UK charts, though it only reached No. 2 in the US.

With Plant now fit again, the band went into intensive rehearsals for an American tour early in 1977 that was planned to be their biggest so far.

'I love rock'n'roll. Sometimes I feel like I was born in the wrong decade because I love Led Zeppelin and Jimi Hendrix – those are my bands.' **MARISA MILLER**

1977 : The Cracks : Begin to Show

T he year started badly for the band: postponed shows, violent altercations on tour, but worse was to come when personal tragedy struck Robert Plant.

Damned and Delayed

Led Zeppelin put the final spit and polish to their act in a converted cinema in Fulham during January, with Page and Plant taking time out to sample the changing musical fashion by going to see punk pioneers The Damned at London's Roxy Club. They got the short, sharp message that The Damned delivered onstage although they did not respond by shortening Led Zeppelin's marathon three-hour set.

In February, just days before the band were due to fly to America to begin their first tour there in two years, Plant went down with tonsillitis and the dates had to be postponed.

Louder and Rowdier

The tour eventually kicked off at the beginning of April in Dallas and the band made their way across America in stages, staying in one city and commuting to their shows on their own plane. Page was frequently looking frail, and a Chicago show was ended after an hour when he fell ill. Their popularity was greater than ever – they broke their own record for the largest attendance for a single band when 76,229 fans packed into the Pontiac Stadium, and played six nights in each of New York and Los Angeles. However, the crowds were getting rowdier, hurling firecrackers around

'All this success and fame. What is it worth? It doesn't mean very much when you compare it to the love of a family.'

ROBERT PLANT'S FATHER

with little regard for their or the band's safety. In Cincinnati, police made over 100 arrests after a thousand ticketless fans stormed the gates, and a show in Tampa to replace one stopped by torrential rain was cancelled after fans went on the rampage.

Violence and Tragedy

The tour all came crashing down on 23 July at San Francisco's Oakland Coliseum, when one of promoter Bill Graham's security staff was beaten to a pulp and hospitalized by Bonham, manager Grant and their bodyguard John Bindon when he refused to let Grant's son unscrew the band's nameplate from their dressing-room door. The next night's show went ahead after Graham was made to sign a letter of indemnification, an illegal act as he had no right to do so on behalf of an employee.

The following morning, police arrived at the band's hotel as they were preparing to leave and arrested the three men plus Richard Cole, charging them all with battery. They were freed on bail and on 26 July flew on to New Orleans for the next show, where Plant received a telephone call from his wife to say that their five-year-old son Karac was seriously ill with a

'My style of singing has always been referred to as "soul" singing when it fact it's more influenced by English R&B Blues Shouting. I'm closer to Led Zeppelin as a vocalist than to Ella Fitzgerald. It was torture dealing with major labels.'

ALISON MOYET

mysterious stomach infection. His condition worsened and he died the following day before he reached hospital. Plant flew home immediately and the remaining seven shows were cancelled. Led Zeppelin would not play in America again.

'...probably at around 17 – my interests switched from hard rock to punk rock. And then by 20 they were circling out of punk rock back into Black Sabbath, Led Zeppelin, the stuff that I didn't get to when I was younger.'

RICK RUBIN

1978-79: Rock Gods Return

Led Zeppelin spent the rest of 1977 and most of 1978 lying low as rumours swirled that they were breaking up; these were finally dispelled when the band made a triumphant live return at the UK's Knebworth Festival in summer 1979.

Lying Low

While the members of Led Zeppelin stayed out of sight for the next year, Page surfaced to deny numerous reports that the band was splitting. He also had to deal with darker rumours

'Led Zeppelin – you just can't find a better band to pay homage to.' ANN WILSON

Robert Plant with his daughter, Carmen Plant, Knebworth 1979.

'Everything I ever learned about rock, I learned from Led Zeppelin.' **MYLES KENNEDY**

that Led Zeppelin had reaped 'bad karma' from his interest in the occult and his ownership of Boleskine House on the shores of Loch Ness, previously owned by Aleister Crowley.

Nobody was pushing Plant to return to work before he felt ready and Page busied himself going through his archive of live tapes amassed over the previous decade, aiming to compile a 'proper' live album. Grant, meanwhile, was dealing with the assault charges hanging over him, Bonham and Cole that were hampering the band's prospects of returning to America.

Speculation over Led Zeppelin's future finally ended when the band flew to Sweden in December 1978 to record at Abba's Polar Studios. It would be notable for the emergence of Jones as the band's musical driving force. His moody synthesizers set the tone for much of the album. While the band could still summon up the fire for archetypal rockers like 'In the Evening', it was the low-key but atmospheric collaboration between Jones and Plant, 'All My Love', that generated more interest.

Knebworth Festival

In May 1979, Led Zeppelin announced their live return with their first British show in four years at the annual Knebworth Festival, 30 miles north of London, in August. They warmed up with a couple of unofficial Danish shows in Copenhagen – where they'd played their first shows together as the New Yardbirds.

On 4 August, they stepped out onstage at Knebworth before more than 100,000 fans, headlining a show that

'Good records – from where I grew up which was listening to Led Zeppelin and Jethro Tull, was about bands that were pushing the envelope a little, musically and in production.' **KIP WINGER**

Festival crowds at the Led Zeppelin concert, Knebworth, 1979.

included Todd Rundgren's Utopia and Fairport Convention. They'd shipped in 100,000 watts of sound and 600,000 watts of lighting, in addition to lasers that literally encased Page during his solo spots in the three-hour show that encompassed songs from across their career, including a couple of brand new ones. Such was the demand that a repeat performance was staged the following week, with the New Barbarians featuring Keith Richards and Ron Wood as special guests.

In Through the Out Door

When Led Zeppelin's new album, *In Through the Out Door*, was released a couple of weeks later, it got generally positive reviews and became their eighth consecutive album to top the UK charts. In the US, the album also stormed to No. 1, where it stayed for a record-breaking seven weeks. It sparked a resurgence of interest in the band and at one point all nine of the band's albums were in the chart despite there being no US tour on the horizon.

'I always wanted to be in Led Zeppelin.' DANNY BOYLE

103

1980: The End

L ed Zeppelin's return at the Knebworth Festival showed that demand for the band was as high as ever, and in the summer of 1980, they embarked on a European tour. But in September at the start of rehearsals for a US tour, the band suffered a blow from which they would not recover.

Back by Popular Demand

The Knebworth Festival was Led Zeppelin's only official show of 1979 – something they had confirmed in advance – but interest in the band immediately shot up to the levels of

'In Led Zeppelin you had four master musicians.'

JIMMY PAGE

their mid-Seventies heyday. Readers of UK music magazine *Record Mirror* voted Knebworth the 'Best Gig' of 1979, while in the US, *Circus* readers voted them 'Best Group', 'Best Guitarist', 'Best Male Singer', 'Best Drummer', 'Best Album', 'Best Songwriters', 'Best Producer' and 'Comeback of the Year'. Not to be outdone, the readers of *Creem* put them at the top in 15 categories.

European Tour

With the assault charges from their San Francisco show three years earlier now settled, the band could make plans to tour America again. They decided to prepare with a European tour in the summer, but when tour manager Cole, whose drug addiction had spiralled out of control, was fired by Grant, it was a warning the band did not heed.

'They sound alright. Jimmy Page has always been a bloody good guitar player.'

JOHN LENNON

'Led Zeppelin has been there through three generations of teenage angst. And there's a generation of kids now who won't know it, post-Linkin Park.' ROBERT PLANT

There was none of the riotous mayhem that had characterized Led Zeppelin tours on their European dates, which dispensed with the flashy lights and special effects and concentrated on the music. However, a frail-looking Page and a stocky, heavily bearded Bonham both appeared unfit. Two weeks into the tour, Bonham collapsed onstage in Nuremberg after three numbers and the show was cancelled. The tour continued without further interruption, although three French dates at the end of the tour were cancelled without explanation. Bonham seemed happy enough though; 'Overall everyone has been dead chuffed with the way this tour's gone,' he said. The band then took a two-month summer break.

'The band didn't exist the minute Bonzo had gone, to me.'

ROBERT PLANT

Bonham's Death

On 24 September, the band gathered at Page's recently acquired Windsor house to start rehearsals for an American tour due to start the following month. Bonham had already been drinking before he arrived and continued for the rest of the day, eventually passing out around midnight. He was found dead in his bed the following afternoon. Plant dashed back to Worcestershire to comfort Bonham's family. He then returned to his own family, where his new son was now eighteen months old. There was then a stunned silence from the band, as if they were unable to comprehend the latest tragedy that had befallen them.

An inquest into Bonham's death on 8 October determined that he had suffocated on his own vomit after drinking more than 40 shots of vodka in 12 hours. Two days later, he was cremated after a private funeral near his farm. Meanwhile, the media, instead of trying to split the band up, linked almost everyone who had ever held a pair of drumsticks with the vacant position in the band. Finally, in early December, the band issued a statement expressing the depth of their loss and concluded by saying: 'We could not continue as we were.' Led Zeppelin was over.

What They Did Next

I n the aftermath of Led Zeppelin both Page and Plant gradually put their solo careers together, reuniting with Jones as a band on three occasions. The last brought lucrative offers for a more permanent reunion, but these have been resisted.

Reledded

Not surprisingly, the three remaining members of Led Zeppelin took time out to reconsider their next moves. Jones retreated back to his family before accepting producing and arranging projects. Page was involved in an abortive plan to form a band with former Yes members in 1981, before recording the soundtrack to *Deathwish II* and compiling an album of leftover Led Zeppelin tracks called *Coda*, released in 1982. He made his live return in I983 at the ARMS multiple sclerosis charity shows in England and America with fellow former Yardbirds Jeff Beck and Eric Clapton.

'I had to get away from it.
It was too heavy. Beautiful,
but talk about examining
your own mortality! Crazy!'

ROBERT PLANT ON THE O2 CONCERT

Plant meanwhile briefly considered abandoning music for teaching, before being encouraged into a solo career by Phil Collins, who was well qualified to help. He put together a band of largely unknown musicians and released *Pictures at Eleven* in 1982 and *The Principle of Moments* the following year, which yielded the 'Big Log' hit single.

In 1984, Page and Plant hooked up in the Honeydrippers and released an EP of rockabilly favourites. It was done strictly for fun. In 1985, all three former Led Zeppelin members answered the call from Bob Geldof and reunited for Live Aid, recruiting Chic and Power Station drummer Tony Thompson plus Phil Collins. But none of them was satisfied with their performance, which they refused to allow on the subsequent DVD.

At Live Aid, 1985, with Phil Collins on drums.

Unledded

Returning to their solo careers, Page teamed up with ex-Free/Bad Company singer Paul Rodgers, releasing a couple of albums as The Firm. He released his first solo album, *Outrider*, in 1988 with contributions from Plant, who had released his third solo album, *Shaken 'N' Stirred*, in 1985 followed by 1988's *Now and Zen*, on which Page guested.

All three answered the call again in 1988, this time from Atlantic Records looking for a headliner for their 40th-anniversary concert at New York's Madison Square Gardens. This time they recruited Bonham's son Jason on drums and, while their performance was better, there was no thought of extending the reunion.

Page teamed up with ex-Deep Purple singer David Coverdale and Plant continued his solo career with *Manic Nirvana* (1990) and *Fate of Nations* (1993) before they were tempted back together by MTV, who offered to fly them to Morocco and reconfigure their Led Zeppelin past with North African musicians. It was an offer they couldn't refuse. *No Quarter – Jimmy Page and Robert Plant Unledded* (1994) was an unqualified success. They even took the show on the road. Unfortunately the follow-up, *Walking Back to Clarksdale*

(1988), featuring their first new material together, lacked direction and spirit, and they went their separate ways again.

Celebration Day (One Night Only)

Page occupied himself remastering Led Zeppelin's back catalogue and compiling a live DVD of concert footage plus a live CD of their epic 1972 shows called *How the West Was Won*, in between playing with Puff Daddy (who had sampled 'Kashmir' on his hit 'Come With Me') and teaming up with the Black Crowes for their *Live at the Greek* album (1999). Meanwhile, Plant shuffled his band around and edged towards Americana, hitting pay dirt when he teamed up with Alison Krauss for the Grammy-award-winning *Raising Sand* album in 2007.

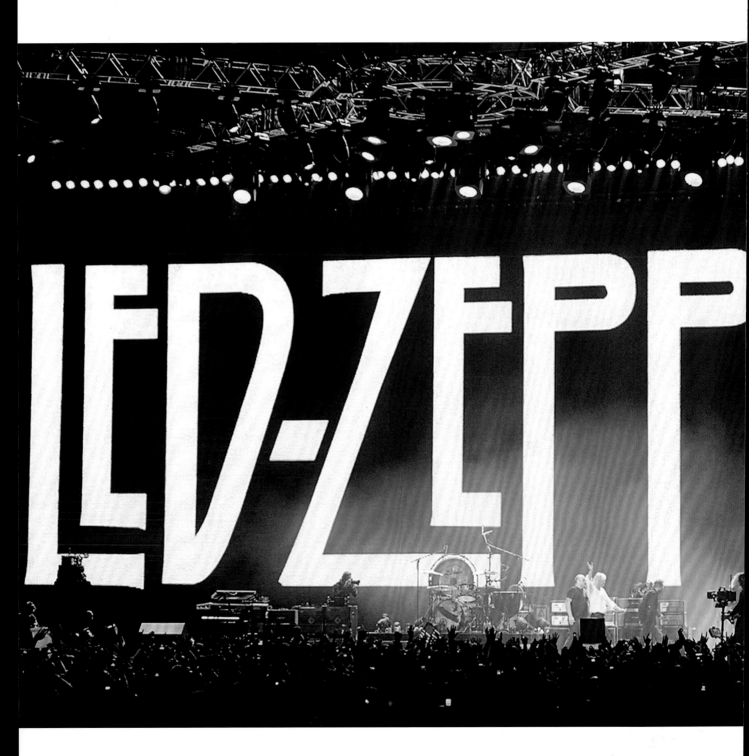

The announcement that Led Zeppelin were reforming for a one-off charity show at London's O2 Arena on 10 December – with Jason Bonham on drums – in honour of the late Atlantic Records president Ahmet Ertegun sent the rock world into a frenzy with 20 million people applying for some 18,000 seats. This time they rehearsed properly and the show was a triumph. Not surprisingly, there were huge offers for the band to tour, but these were resisted – mainly by Plant, who was determined that Led Zeppelin's legacy should not be diluted in any way.

Tribute concert for Ahmet Ertegun, O2, 2007.

'In the run-up to the O2 concert, the only music that we played was … Led Zeppelin – the past catalogue stuff … But we played really, really well.'

JIMMY PAGE

Game Changers

L ed Zeppelin's main legacy is their music, neatly encapsulated in their eight studio albums. But they left something else behind: legends that enhanced their status as the rock gods of the Seventies and ensured their place in rock mythology.

'People are always telling me how important our music has been to their life. And that, really, is the whole heritage and the legacy of Led Zeppelin.' JIMMY PAGE

Rock God Legends

Their reputation in America as swashbuckling British invaders who swept all before them as they conquered the citadels of rock'n'roll chimed perfectly with the new generation of rock fans. These were too young to have seen The Beatles or join the hippy movement and wanted rock heroes of their own to worship. It didn't matter that many of the tales surrounding the group – of young maidens being ravished by the score; of Harley Davidson bikes being ridden down the corridors of their hotel at full throttle; of groupies and orgies in darkened rooms accompanied by a sprinkling of black magic – were

'I love listening to Led Zeppelin and classic rock albums from the Seventies. They're just so brilliant because they breathe.'

ZACKY VENGEANCE (AVENGED SEVENFOLD)

exaggerated. To many of their fans, such debaucheries were believable and simply fired their imaginations.

Onstage, Page and Plant looked the part – Page with his cherubic face ringed by curls and Plant with his cascading blond mane and bare chest, twitching like a sex god as he shimmied across the stage. It seemed far removed from the traditional macho idea of what a heavy-rock group should look like – almost the opposite, in fact – but it carried a fierce potency with which their young fans could identify. Other British heavy-rock bands like Deep Purple and Black Sabbath looked ponderous in comparison.

'Now, when I look back, I don't get any sense of great achievement out of the fact that people still like [the music] a lot. I get achievement out of the fact it was good.' ROBERT PLANT

A Band of Their Time

It's fair to say that most rock critics at the time did not fully understand Led Zeppelin. Most of them came from an earlier era dominated by The Beatles and the Rolling Stones and the hippy culture of the Sixties. To them, rock'n'roll embodied love and peace and challenging the system, particularly when it came to issues like the Vietnam War. Their rock'n'roll heroes deliberately raised social awareness – Bob Dylan ('Blowing In The Wind'), the Rolling Stones ('Street Fighting Man') and John Lennon ('Give Peace A Chance').

Led Zeppelin and other bands who rose to fame in the Seventies were less concerned with social revolution. Instead, they offered an escape from reality. The venues they played became shrines to the new rock'n'roll religion. Gathered together en masse, the fans responded with a fervour that was equally religious in its intensity.

Bad Times, Good Times

In an era before computer games, MTV or YouTube, rock'n'roll took on a special significance, because adult generations reacted with suspicion. To rock fans growing up

in the Seventies, this simply increased its allure – something that could symbolize their rebellious spirit.

By the end of the Seventies, punk rock had arrived to upset the apple cart again. Only the best bands survived the cull. Had Led Zeppelin not been struck down by the tragic death of their drummer, they would have undoubtedly survived into the Eighties. They had already seen the challenge of punk and they relished it. As it is, they still stand intact as the supreme icon of Seventies heavy rock.

'I remember that poster of Led Zeppelin with the plane. I had it on my wall when I was a kid. I thought that was the coolest.'

DAVID BRYAN

Further Information
Led Zeppelin Vital Info

Jimmy Page

Birth Name:	James Patrick Page
Birth Date:	9 January 1944
Birthplace:	Heston, Middlesex, England
Role:	Guitarist, songwriter

Robert Plant

Birth Name:	Robert Anthony Plant
Birth Date:	20 August 1948
Birthplace:	West Bromwich, Staffordshire, England
Role:	Lead singer, lyricist

John Paul Jones

Birth Name:	John Richard Baldwin
Birth Date:	3 January 1946
Birthplace:	Sidcup, Kent, England
Role:	Bass player, keyboardsr

John Bonham

Birth Name:	John Henry Bonham
Birth & Death Dates:	31 May 1948–25 September 1980
Birthplace:	Redditch, Worcestershire, England
Role:	Drummer

Discography
Studio Albums

Led Zeppelin (1969): No. 6 UK, No. 10 US

Led Zeppelin II (1969): No. 1 UK, No. 1 US

Led Zeppelin III (1970): No. 1 UK, No. 1 US

Led Zeppelin IV (1971): No. 1 UK, No. 2 US

Houses of the Holy (1973): No. 1 UK, No. 1 US

Physical Graffiti (1975): No. 1 UK, No. 1 US

Presence (1976): No. 1 UK, No. 2 US

In Through the Out Door (1979): No. 1 UK, No. 1 US

Led Zeppelin Stats

No. of records sold worldwide:
300 million (and counting)

Most weeks on US album chart:
281 *(Led Zeppelin IV)*

Most weeks on UK album chart: 129 (Led Zeppelin II)

No. of UK consecutive No. 1s: 8

First band to have six albums on *Billboard* chart simultaneously: 29 March 1975

No. of Diamond Awards (certified US sales of over 10 million): 5

Size of crowd at 1979 Knebworth Festival: 200,000

Date Led Zeppelin broke The Beatles' concert attendance record: 5 May 1973 (56,800), Tampa, Florida

Most famous song never to be released as a single:
'Stairway to Heaven' (1971)

Date new rock-concert earnings record was set: 30 April 1977. $800,000. Pontiac Stadium, Michigan.

Cost of making *Led Zeppelin I*: £1,782

Other Albums (selected)

The Song Remains The Same (1976): movie soundtrack;
No. 1 UK, No. 2 US

How the West Was Won (2003): live triple album;
   No. 5 UK, No. 1 US

Celebration Day: concert film; UK No. 4, US No. 5

Coda (1982): compilation; UK No. 4, US No. 6

Led Zeppelin Boxed Set (1990)

Led Zeppelin Remasters (1990): compilation; UK No. 10

Mothership (2007): compilation; UK No. 4, US No. 7

Online

www.ledzeppelin.com

Official site of the Rock God legends.

www.youtube.co.uk/user/ledzeppelin

Band's official YouTube channel, with archival footage, videos and more.

twitter.com/ledzeppelin

Visit this site to join in with the Led Zeppelin twitterati.

www.tightbutloose.co.uk

Online site of Led Zeppelin fan magazine, *Tight But Loose.*

ledzepnews.com

For all the latest (unofficial) Led Zeppelin news.

Biographies

Hugh Fielder (Author)

In 1963 Hugh Fielder was about to bunk off school to see the Rolling Stones when he was 'advised' that a formal request would be granted in exchange for an essay. His future career was established, although he didn't know it at the time. He arrived in London in 1966 and spent his student years following Cream, Jimi Hendrix and The Who around town and soaking up the pop culture. He worked for *Sounds* and *TOP*, enjoying a front-row seat on the rock scene during that time. He is regular contributor to *Classic Rock*, amongst other publication, and has written books on the Beatles, Pink Floyd, The Police, Genesis, Queen and Lady Gaga.

Dave Lewis (Foreword)

Dave Lewis is acknowledged and respected throughout the world as a leading chronicler of Led Zeppelin and its individual members. He is the author of several Led Zeppelin books and the editor of the acclaimed long running Led Zeppelin magazine and website *Tight But Loose.* Visit www.tightbutloose.co.uk for further details.

Picture Credits